D0712252

REGINA PUBLIC LIBRARY

by Wendy Perkins

Consulting Editor: Gail Saunders-Smith, PhD

Consultant: Jennifer Zablotny, DVM
Member, American Veterinary Medical Association

Capstone
press®

Mankato, Minnesota

Pebble Books are published by Capstone Press,
151 Good Counsel Drive, P.O. Box 669, Mankato, Minnesota 56002.
www.capstonepress.com

Copyright © 2008 by Capstone Press, a Capstone Publishers company.
All rights reserved.
No part of this publication may be reproduced in whole or in part,
or stored in a retrieval system, or transmitted in any form or by any means,
electronic, mechanical, photocopying, recording, or otherwise,
without written permission of the publisher.
For information regarding permission, write to Capstone Press,
151 Good Counsel Drive, P.O. Box 669, Dept. R, Mankato, Minnesota 56002.
Printed in the United States of America

1 2 3 4 5 6 13 12 11 10 09 08

Library of Congress Cataloging-in-Publication Data
Perkins, Wendy, 1957–
    Maine coon cats / by Wendy Perkins.
    p. cm. — (Pebble books. Cats)
    Includes bibliographical references and index.
    ISBN-13: 978-1-4296-1216-6 (hardcover)
    ISBN-10: 1-4296-1216-9 (hardcover)
    1. Maine coon cat — Juvenile literature. I. Title. II. Series.
SF449.M34P47 2008
636.8′3 — dc22   2007017793

Summary: Simple text and photographs present an introduction to the Maine Coon
breed, its growth from kitten to adult, and pet care information.

Note to Parents and Teachers

The Cats set supports national science standards related to life
science. This book describes and illustrates Maine Coon cats.
The images support early readers in understanding the text. The
repetition of words and phrases helps early readers learn new
words. This book also introduces early readers to subject-specific
vocabulary words, which are defined in the Glossary section. Early
readers may need assistance to read some words and to use the
Table of Contents, Glossary, Read More, Internet Sites, and Index
sections of the book.

Table of Contents

Curious Cats

Maine Coons are friendly
and curious cats.
Maine Coons make
good pets.

Maine Coons are big cats.
They have long, fluffy coats.

8

A Maine Coon wraps
its tail around its body
to stay warm.

From Kitten to Adult

Newborn Maine Coons
can't walk.
They scoot on their bellies
toward their mother.

Kittens walk on
wobbly legs after
about three weeks.

Maine Coons are
fully grown after
three to five years.

Caring for Maine Coons

Maine Coons lick
their coats to keep clean.
Owners should brush their
Maine Coons every day.

18

Maine Coons need water and cat food every day. Hard, crunchy food helps keep their teeth clean.

Maine Coons like being with people.
Maine Coons love sitting near their owners.

Glossary

coat — a cat's fur

curious — eager to explore and learn about new things

fluffy — covered with soft, fine hair

friendly — kind

owner — a person who has something; pets need owners who care for them.

scoot — to slide across a surface

wobbly — unsteady

Read More

Barnes, Julia. *Pet Cats.* Pet Pals. Milwaukee: Gareth Stevens, 2007.

Loves, June. *Cats.* Pets. Philadelphia: Chelsea Clubhouse, 2004.

Shores, Erika L. *Caring for Your Cat.* First Facts. Positively Pets. Mankato, Minn.: Capstone Press, 2007.

Internet Sites

FactHound offers a safe, fun way to find Internet sites related to this book. All of the sites on FactHound have been researched by our staff.

Here's how:

1. Visit *www.facthound.com*

2. Choose your grade level.

3. Type in this book **ID 1429612169** for age-appropriate sites. You may also browse subjects by clicking on letters, or by clicking on pictures and words.

4. Click on the **Fetch It** button.

FactHound will fetch the best sites for you!

Index

Word Count: 112
Grade: 1
Early-Intervention Level: 16

Editorial Credits
Erika L. Shores, editor; Renée T. Doyle, set designer; Veronica Bianchini
    and Ted Williams, contributing designers; Linda Clavel, photo researcher

Photo Credits
Chanan Photography, 8
Fiona Green, 4, 14, 16, 20
iStockphoto/Magoral, cover, 1, 22
Norvia Behling/Connie Summers, 6, 18
Rona Magnay, 10, 12
Shutterstock/Florea Marius Catalin, 18 (food)

Capstone Press thanks Rona Magnay of www.catswhiskers.uk.com.